Being Your Own Best Friend

(Feeling Good To Be Me)

You Always Have Other Options
Which one will you choose?

Written by
Janine Fletcher

Book illustrations by

_____

(Write your own name here)

Where you see a picture frame, draw a picture about what you've just read.

DISCLAIMER

The suggestions in this book for personal growth are not meant to substitute for the advice of a trained professional such as a medical doctor, psychologist, therapist etc. It is essential to consult such a professional in the case of any physical or mental symptoms.

Being Your Own Best Friend

YAHOO Feel Good Series

Being Your Own Best Friend
(Feeling Good To Be Me)

Feeling Good On The Inside
(Feeling Good To Be Alive)

What A Wonderful World
(Feeling Good To Live In This World)

Do you know that you have someone with you every minute of every day for your whole entire life?

When you go to bed at night   ...that someone is with you.

When you wake up in the morning ... that someone is with you.

When you go to school or play with your friends   ... that someone is with you.

All through the day and all through the night, no matter what you do, no matter where you go   ... that someone is with you.

Can you guess who that someone is?

It's not your mum
It's not your dad.
It's not your teacher.
It's not your brother or your sister.
It's not your nana or your pop.
It's not even your best friend.

Can you guess who is with you every minute of every day for your whole entire life?

It's YOU!

You are the only person who is with you every minute of every day for your whole entire life.

When you go to bed at night   ...there you are.

When you wake up in the morning   ... there you are.

When you go to school or play with your friends   ... there you are.

All through the day and all through the night, no matter what you do, no matter where you go   ... there you are.

Do you also know that you can be your own best friend or your own worst enemy?

Let me explain.

Where you see a picture frame, draw a picture about what you've just read.

A best friend is kind to you, likes you, is fun to be with, and says nice things to you and it feels good to be around them.

When you're being your own best friend you say things to yourself like,

> "I can do it."
>
> "Have a go."
>
> "I did a good job."
>
> "I'm fun to be with".
>
> "I like myself".
>
> "I'm kind."
>
> "I don't worry if I make a mistake, I just have another go."
>
> "Someone will help."
>
> "Everything will be o.k."

It **feels good to be you** when you're being your own best friend.

A worst enemy is someone who is mean to you, is not fun to be with, says unkind things to you and it doesn't feel good to be with them.

When you're being your own worst enemy you say things to yourself like,
> "I can't do it."
> "It's no use trying."
> "I'm dumb."
> "I hate myself."
> "Nobody likes me."
> "Everyone will laugh at me."
> "No one will help me."
> "Nothing good ever happens to me."

It **doesn't feel good to be you** when you're being your own worst enemy.

When you feel good you have lots of energy, you want to join in, you have lots of fun, you are kind to others, people want to be around you and it **feels good to be you!**

The bad news is that sometimes you can forget that to *feel good to be you*, you need to be your own best friend.

The good news is that your body has a special way of talking to you that will help you to remember.

You already know some of the ways your body talks to you,

>When you are hungry your tummy will rumble.

>When you are thirsty your mouth will feel dry.

>When you are tired you will yawn.

This is your body's way of letting you know that you need to eat, drink or sleep.

Your body also has a special way of letting you know when you are being your own worst enemy.

When you're being your own worst enemy and saying unkind things to yourself,

>It will be hard to breathe properly.

>...Sometimes you might even stop breathing!!

>The area around your tummy will feel all tense, tight and closed.

>Your body will slouch and your head will hang down.

>You will feel sad or angry inside.

>You will have a frown on your face.

All of these things are your **body talking to you** and it is telling you that you are being your own worst enemy.

Your body also has a special way of letting you know when you are being your own best friend.

When you're being your own best friend and saying kind things to yourself,

> You will breathe easily and deeply.
> The area around your tummy will feel all relaxed, soft and open.
> You will stand up straight and tall.
> You will feel happy or peaceful inside.
> You will have a smile on your face.

All of these things are your **body talking to you** and it is telling you that you are being your own best friend.

Everyone you know, everyone who has a body, their body is talking to them all the time.

> Your mum's body talks to your mum.
>
> Your dad's body talks to your dad.
>
> Your teacher's body talks to your teacher.
>
> Your brother's body talks to your brother.
>
> Your sister's body talks to your sister.
>
> Your best friend's body talks to your best friend

Everyone's body will talk to them. It will let them know when they are being their own worst enemy but not everyone knows what to do to stop being their own worst enemy. When you learn what you need to do to stop being your own worst enemy it's as easy as 1, 2, 3!

All you have to do is take ten slow, deep breaths all the way down into your tummy and say something kind to yourself like, 'everything will be o.k.', 'someone will help me', 'I'm doing a good job'.

It's as easy as 1, 2, 3.

1. Your body talks to you and lets you know that you're being your own worst enemy.
2. Take 10 slow, deep breaths all the way down into your tummy.
3. Say something kind to yourself.

Let's practise doing this now...

Pretend you just made a mistake in your drawing. You say something mean to yourself, like 'I'm so dumb, I've wrecked the whole thing.'

1. Your body talks to you and lets you know that you're being your own worst enemy.
2. Take 10 slow, deep breaths, all the way down into your tummy.
3. Say something kind to yourself, like 'It's ok. I have an even better idea. My next drawing will be better.'

Pretend a friend just said that they don't want to play with you. You say something mean to yourself like, 'Nobody likes me. There must be something wrong with me.'

1. Your body talks to you and lets you know that you're being your own worst enemy.
2. Take 10 slow, deep breaths, all the way down into your tummy.
3. Say something kind to yourself like, 'I wonder who else I can play with today. I will make another friend.'

Pretend someone just beat you in a race. You say something mean to yourself like, 'I'll never be as good as him. He's better than me.'

1. Your body talks to you and lets you know that you're being your own worst enemy.
2. Take 10 slow, deep breaths, all the way down into your tummy.
3. Say something kind to yourself like, 'I did my best. If I practise I can get faster.'

To *feel good to be you* remember it's as easy as 1, 2, 3. B.B.B.

1. **B**ody talk
2. **B**reathe (all the way down into your tummy)
3. **B**est friend

So, when you go to bed at night … make sure you have your best friend with you.

When you wake up in the morning … make sure you have your best friend with you.

When you go to school or play with your friends … make sure you have your best friend with you.

All through the day and all through the night… No matter what you do. No matter where you go …

 … Make sure you have your best friend with you.

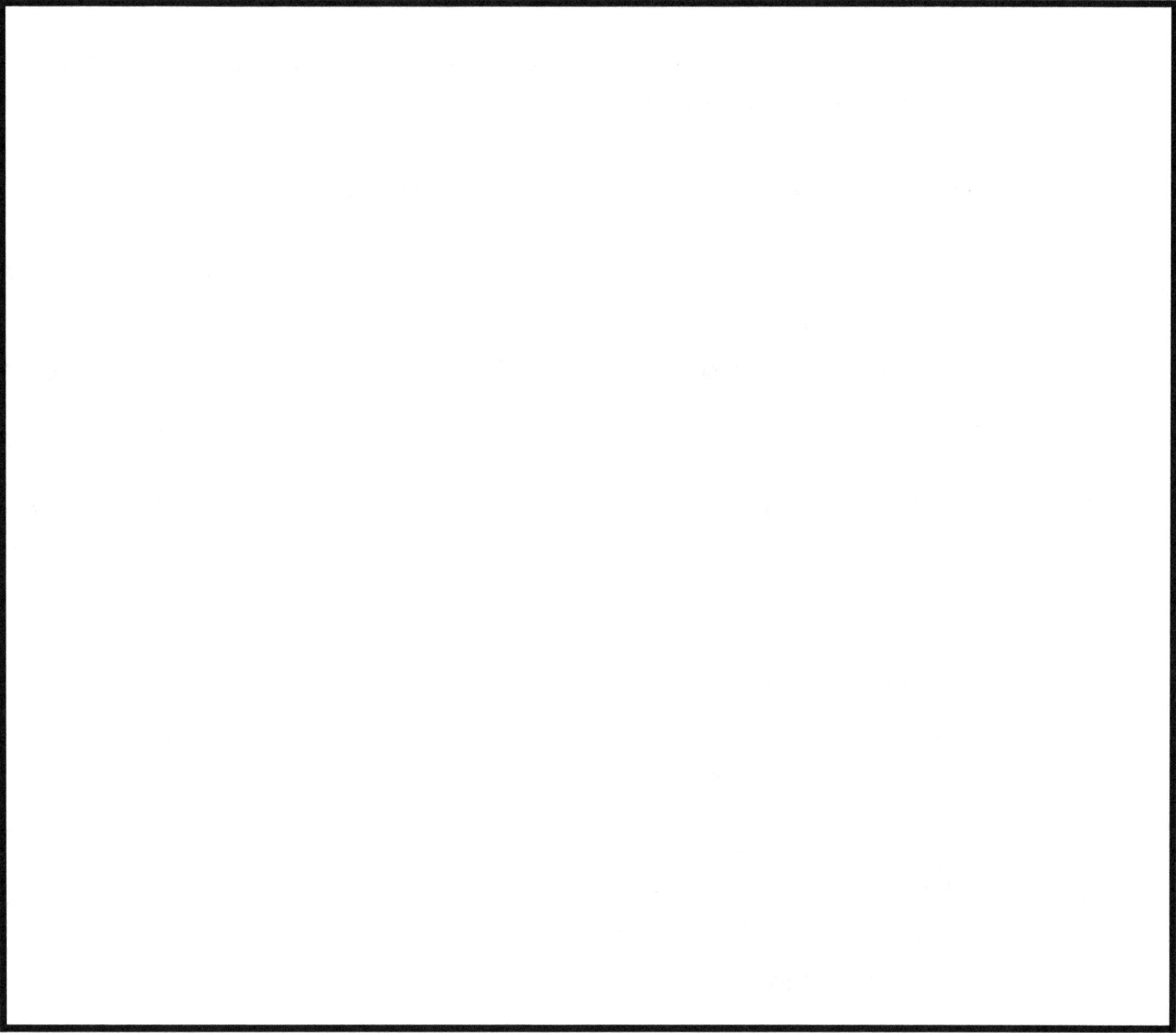

The more you have your best friend with you, the better you will feel and pretty soon it will **feel great to be you!**

To **feel good to be you**, remember it's as easy as 1, 2, 3. B.B.B.

1. **B**ody talk. Your body talks to you and lets you know that you're being your own worst enemy.
2. **B**reathe. Take 10 slow, deep breaths, all the way down into your tummy.
3. **B**est friend. Say something kind to yourself.

Here is a list of things that you can say to yourself that will help you to be your own best friend.

"I'm great."

"I love being me."

"I like being my own best friend."

"I can do it."

"Just do my best."

"I like the way I did that."

"I will get better if I practise."

"I'm a kind friend."

"Ask someone to help me."

"If I make a mistake, I'll just have another go."

"Everything will be o.k."

"I did a good job."

"I'm really good at ...."

Write some of your own words that you can say to yourself to be your own best friend ...

_____   _____

_____   _____

_____   _____

_____   _____

_____   _____

_____   _____

I wonder if your body talks to you the same way when you are being a friend or an enemy to other people?

Let's do some pretending to see if we can find out.

Pretend that you are really angry with someone and you say something mean to them like, "I hate you!"

Notice what happens to your body.

Notice what happens to your breathing, the area around your tummy, how you feel inside, and what your face looks like.

Did you notice that if you get angry with someone *your body feels* the anger-?

> It is hard to breathe properly.
> The area around your tummy feels all tight, tense and closed.
> You feel angry inside.
> You have a mean look on your face.

Wow, isn't that interesting!

When you are being mean to someone else your body talks to you exactly the same way as when you are being mean to yourself.

Now let's pretend that you are being really kind to someone and you say something kind to them like, "Would you like me to help you?"

Notice what happens to your body.

Notice what happens to your breathing, the area around your tummy, how you feel inside, and what your face looks like.

Did you notice that if you are kind to someone *your body feels* the kindness-?

      Your breathing is soft and deep.
      The area around your tummy feels all relaxed, soft and open.
      You feel kind inside.
      You have a smile on your face.

Wow, isn't that interesting!

When you are being kind to someone else your body talks to you exactly the same way as when you are being kind to yourself.

Being mean to someone else is just the same as being mean to yourself, and being kind to someone else is just the same as being kind to yourself.

This works with everything.

Here are some other things you can try...

Think about how much you love someone in your family. Did you feel the love in your body? Did it feel like you were being your own best friend or your own worst enemy?

Think about having a fight with someone. Did you feel the fight in your body? Did it feel like you were being your own best friend or your own worst enemy?

Think about having fun and playing with your friends. Did you feel the play and fun in your body? Did it feel like you were being your own best friend or your own worst enemy?

Think about being mean to someone and making fun of them. Did you feel the meanness in your body? Did it feel like you were being your own best friend or your own worst enemy?

Think about telling a funny story or joke. Did you feel the fun and laughter in your body? Did it feel like you were being your own best friend or your own worst enemy?

So, when you want to *feel good to be you* you can say things to others like,

> "You can do it."
> "Have a go."
> "You did a good job."
> "You're fun to be with".
> "I like you".
> "You're kind."
> "Don't worry if you make a mistake, just have another go."
> "Someone will help."
> "Everything will be o.k."

It *feels good to be you* when you're being a good friend to someone else.

But remember it won't *feel good to be you* if you say things to others like,

> "You can't do it."
> "It's no use trying."
> "You're dumb".
> "I hate you".
> "Nobody likes you"
> "Everyone will laugh at you"
> "No one will help you."
> "Nothing good will ever happen to you."

It doesn't *feel good to be you* when you're being an enemy to someone else. .

Remember...
When you feel love towards another person YOU feel the love
When you feel angry towards another person YOU feel the anger
When you feel kindness towards another person YOU feel the kindness.
When you feel jealousy towards another person YOU feel the jealousy.
When you feel revenge towards another person YOU feel the revenge.
When you feel gratitude towards another person YOU feel the gratitude.

So remember whether you're talking to yourself or to someone else,

It's as easy as 1, 2, 3.

1. Your body talks to you and lets you know that you're being your own or someone else's worst enemy.
2. Take 10 slow, deep breaths, all the way down into your tummy.
3. Say something kind to yourself or someone else.

All through the day and all through the night… No matter what you do. No matter where you go…

… Make sure you have your best friend with you.

The more you have your best friend with you, the better you will feel and pretty soon it will be FEELING **GREAT** TO BE YOU!

To *feel good to be you* remember it's as easy as 1, 2, 3 - B. B. B.

1   **B**ody talk - Your body talks to you and lets you know that you're being a friend or an enemy.
2. **B**reathe - Take 10 slow, deep breaths, all the way down into your tummy.
3. **B**est friend - Say something kind.

Information for Parents and Teachers

The **Yahoo series of 'Feel Good'** books are designed to work at the most fundamental level of how we are neurologically wired; the structure of the human brain.

The neural connections in our brain are formed by repetition and reinforcement. Learning to walk, talk, ride a bike, drive a car, read, write and so on are examples we can easily identify with to understand how we learn to do something.

The more we practise and reinforce any skills, the more automatic they become. When it becomes automatic for us, we no longer have to be conscious of what we're doing, we're just doing it.

Having a positive attitude and learning to feel good about ourselves can be understood in a similar way. As we repeat thoughts, emotions and actions over and over again, they become automatic patterns of behaviour; the way our brain is wired up.

What we may fail to understand is that the brain doesn't discriminate among thoughts on the neurological level. It takes no more effort to form a positive thought than it does a negative one. Attitudes are simply accumulations of related neural nets and positive attitudes are just as easy to construct as negative ones.
(Evolve Your Brain By Joe Dispenza p.449)

Over time, by applying and practising the concepts presented in the 'Yahoo Feel Good' series of books this way of thinking will become the dominant/automatic way of thinking, feeling and acting because it's the way the brain has been wired.

It is recommended that your child illustrate the pages in this book;- as your child is thinking about how to illustrate the concepts presented in the text, it will help stimulate and establish positive neural connections. Each time the story is re read or the concepts discussed, these connections will be activated and reinforced.

With consistent awareness, repetition and reinforcement, these thoughts will become beliefs; embedded in the child's neurology; the structure of their brain.

www.ingramcontent.com/pod-product-compliance
Lightning Source LLC
LaVergne TN
LVHW061341060426
835511LV00014B/2045